Good Girl, Gone Bad, Gone Holy

Finding My Way Back to Myself

By Jennifer Mason

D1568486

COPYRIGHT 2017

Good Girl, Gone Bad, Gone Holy by Jennifer Mason

Copyright © 2017

"Good Girl, Gone Bad, Gone Holy"

ISBN-13: 978-0692828595

Editing and Formatting by Norah Sarsour, NS & Associates, www.writeeditlove.com

Cover Design by Kevin Ransom RansomArtistry.com

Dedication

This memoir is dedicated to my Mommy & sisters they've been my rocks. To every woman who has been on this journey of transformation, & every piece of pain that now is purpose.

Good Girl, Gone Bad, Gone Holy

Acknowledgement

To my parents. Thank you for loving me, shaping me, planting powerful seeds, believing in me and allowing me to be myself. Today I'm so thankful to have you both in my life.

To my sisters. I am your keeper. I love you and pray this book inspires you to be the BEST you possible. I'm here cheering you to the finish line.

To my friends (way too many to name) I love you guys. From childhood, to college, and after college. So many of you have played a vital role in my life. Thank you for being there for me when needed and showing me true friendship exist.

To EVERY Pastor and Mentor. Thank you for being obedient to your call. It's largely because of your "Yes" that I have the testimony I have today.

Good Girl, Gone Bad, Gone Holy

Introduction

They say once a good girl's gone bad, she's gone forever…or is she?

So here I am, finally ready to submit one hundred percent to God—like I am *really* ready this time. I am a self-worth coach.

I'm not writing this book for the judgmental. This book is for those who want to get right after they took the crooked path. I want you to rest assured that you are not alone. There is at least one woman ready to stand and tell the truth and set us all free from the demons that try to take over our lives. The influence of peers can try to interrupt destiny. A lot of women are lost and seek validation through men but not the main man who is God. God is a teacher and mastermind when it comes to the details of our lives.

The next few chapters are going to be different events that I have since encountered in my life. Some stories will make you cry, some will make you laugh, but all in all I want you to learn from my mistakes and strive for my triumphs for yourself and those close to you. We learn not simply for the benefit of ourselves but for them.

Table of Contents

Good Girl, Gone Bad, Gone Holy

Chapter 1: Beginning Blueprint

I wasn't born into the church. I was brought up with great principles though. Respect adults, be kind to each other, remember your manners. That kind of thing. I was a quiet, sweet child. I remember being extremely grateful for the things my mom would afford my life, often saying thank you for everything given to me. I had manners and addressed adults with much respect. I was a normal little girl who just liked playing with her Barbie dolls.

I mean I would play Barbies for hours. My introverted ways were established at a young age, and I really didn't need a crowd to have a good time. I enjoyed my own company. I would play out entire life scenes with my dolls. From having babies, to shopping, or traveling. I had everything Barbie. And I do mean everything!

For a short-lived period when my dad was in my life, I had everything. He took me a few times to church and did plant a large seed which is the fruit of what many see of me today. My dad would anoint my head with oil every time he saw me and my sister. My eldest sister and I have the same dad. He would let me watch the movie, *The Ten Commandments* over and over. It was as a child when I was introduced to the miracle power of God. When God parted the sea for Moses, I was so fascinated! Seeing the sea part before them showed me the power of God. It was a power I had never seen before here on earth. This showed me there was in fact a God.

I also loved watching the movie *Glory*, a war movie. In *Glory* the soldiers faced so much opposition. Through their tenacity and strength, they fought past discouragement and racism. The action in the fighting scenes excited me, but at the same time seeing them die and be injured would make me sad. I loved this movie most because my dad would watch it with me.

Then there was *Thriller* with Michael Jackson. The dancing drew me in. I danced as a child all the way through my senior year in college. I would learn the choreography and would perform the routine while the movie played.

When I look back I see why these movies grabbed my attention. Between my mom and dad, they, instilled my purpose into my life. The movies all give light to who I am. I am called to cast out demons, heal the sick and set people free through warfare. I was chosen just like Moses to bring Glory to God kingdom.

My mother showed me my self-worth, and my dad showed me God. Through the movies, I've learned that I enjoy going to war in Satan's camp, warring againts demons with the power of Jesus Christ.

I was always the young ambitious girl, but I honestly did not know what was good for me. I may have been ambitious, but I was good at what I did for the wrong reasons at times. I got myself my own job at 15 as a dance teacher at my local community center, which we referred to as the *Pal*. I was young but wise. I hung out at the *Pal* often with my friends. I was in dancing most of my life and noticed the program was going to need a new teacher. I didn't even realize how much of an entrepreneur I already was when I asked when the two current teachers were leaving so I could replace one. One told me it was her last year, so I went to the director to claim the position before anyone else. I let him know why I was qualified for the position, and he hired me!

He was impressed with my initiative and maturity. Needless to say, I was 15 making my own hours, teaching dance classes, and having the time of my life. I taught ballet, tap, hip hop-jazz. I determined when I worked and   how much I was paid. Just like I do today.

Chapter 2. Doll Baby Mommas Baby

Jennifer is my name given to me by mom, and unlike my sisters who have very unique names, my name was given because it was the name my mother named her favorite baby-doll. My mother realized back in 1987 that there weren't many black girls named Jennifer, and since it was such a pretty name, she thought a black girl should have it as well.

I actually was a planned pregnancy. I was an easy labor and everything. Three hours, and I was here on this earth. That may have been the only thing that was planned in my life that went that smoothly. The rest was God, honestly.

Mothers are biologically so, and no one can ever take her place. If I could speak from her perspective, I was just the different one out of the three girls she had—not as a favorite, but my personality was just different. I was the easiest birth, I barely cried, I was the brown baby, and I just was, and have been, different.

My mother is an amazingly strong woman. I remember being super young playing with dolls in my playroom with my oldest sister. My mother would come in and preach to us—not like a pastor, don't trip. She would let us know the importance of making sure a man brought something to the table. Now, she wasn't turning us into gold diggers, she was preparing us to NEVER be taken advantage of by a man. She wanted us to be sure we knew that a man provides his half of the deal. We had heartbreaks yes, however there was a strong standard set that not just any man

5

could have us. We are jewels in her eyes, and any man who couldn't see us the same needed to "get da stepping."

All single moms are the real MVPS. I watched my mom make so many sacrifices in order to see my sisters and I happy. My mother sacrificed her wants and needs just so I could make it to dance rehearsals, and I'm sure much more than she has never told us. Although my dad wasn't present as much as I would have liked, my mother definitely carried the weight of motherhood with class and grace. My mother was a single mom for a good portion of my childhood but did thankfully have support from a later husband we lovingly called "Buddy."

I'm much older now, and as I have grown in God, I've grown in honor. The word says to honor your parents. I didn't always agree with my mother and Father growing up either I mean what child does. We can come out the womb thinking we know it all, But I came out great because of her push. She made sure to allow me to spread my wings. When people came up against me she defended me. I wouldn't be half the woman I am without her today.

Who would've shown me how to go after my dreams and it was never too late? Who would've shown me strength in a storm? Who would've been there when everyone else left? Who would've picked out my fake friends when my loyalty held me in bondage? Who would've helped me plan a wedding she didn't 100% agree with but didn't want to hurt my feeling so she went with it?

There wasn't much we went without honestly. It takes a strong woman to make this happen and I am appreciative of all her sacrifices. Mothers are so special and even though I know there's no way I could pay her back, my plan is to truly show her that I understand.

Cherish your mothers you only get one. Pray for them, and always love them exactly for who they are.

Now was I an angel? Most days I may have been. I was a young girl from NJ with a whole lot of attitude and ambition. That didn't always go over well with the other girls I hung out with. For a great portion of my childhood thing were normal—girls playing double-dutch, hide and seek, doing each other's hair, and of course, Barbies.

I was never the promiscuous type. I actually was the friend who kept her virginity when all her friends were losing theirs in the 8th grade. I would kiss boys on the back roads with my friends, but I wasn't letting them into my jewelry box, as my mother so lovingly would refer to it. My mother drove self-worth into my heart heavily at a young age and even still through adult hood.

She always said, "If he isn't bringing anything to the table he need not have a seat" or "don't go to bed with a wet behind and wake up with a dry palm."

I learned quickly that when you start excelling, those around you can't always handle it. We ended up splitting ways. I went off to college in NC and started a new life with a few others from high school but not my immediate crew—except one person, my best friend.

Never would I have thought that I'd bring a lot of anger from New Jersey with me to NC. I thought I was over the past I left in New Jersey.

I became known as "Juju with All That Mouth." I let all the anger I held back take over and got into a lot of messes. Naturally always having my guard up, I felt I had to fight my way out of everything. I was young and foolish. I wouldn't fight clean either, I had been carrying a weapon since high school. College was no different.

I remember a young lady who didn't care for come for me and long story short when they tried to jump me a few of them got a box cutter to meet them followed by a punch or three. My best friend, a guy, ended up having to help. Needless to say, one young lady got knocked out by a man. I don't condone this of course, but it happened. And back then I didn't care and neither did he.

Don't come for me.

And that's just how he felt.

I could've applied to local schools but I refused to give myself an option to stay—kind of like where I am currently in my life. I am not giving myself an option to go back to who I was.

I was off to North Carolina. I had no clue what I was in for but my excitement led me without fear. I was free, had my own "spot" (dorm room), and my mother couldn't come knocking on my door anymore.

Freedom.

So, I thought.

As I went off to college, broken on the inside but *ready* for what was to come, I knew that God had plan.

I was like, "NJ, I am out of here."

And I never looked back. I left NJ in August of 2005, the state where I was born and raised, and set off for college. A new world was awaiting me! I was hoping to escape the drama and start fresh.

Needless to say, my last few years in NJ were HELL! I truly was on the search for peace. I moved on and started a new chapter of my life.

Jennifer, do you have everything you need for school on that list?'

Yes, mommy. Time to hit the road.

.

Chapter 3. Angel Armies

T he girls I called my friends, even my best friends, turned on me. All except one. It was a number of things at that age, from jealousy to just obeying the "leader" and them expecting me to hop on the bandwagon. We would fight right in front of the house, full out brawls, one side of the street against the other. I was terrified, but I had to defend myself. I mean everyone was watching, and I couldn't back down, right?

My mom was backing me up, letting me know it was ok to handle my business. I wish someone would've sat us all down and talked sense and unity into our hard skulls, showed the value of friendship, and reminded us that the decisions we made could harm us in the future.

I remember sitting outside one day and the eldest cousin came in and punch me right in my face, when I was sitting on a car, in front of my home. My face was throbbing and I was enraged. That started another brawl. They got so bad, we had to have cameras in front of our house in the window. The police wouldn't arrest anyone without proof. Silly, I know. Ripped clothing and black eyes weren't enough proof. I couldn't even walk out of my home in peace without being called some name or being threatened. It was hell just to be home, and to leave meant I had to prepare for battle.

That's not where it ended either. I was the captain of my cheerleading squad and my best friend was the majorette of the band. As we left the game one day, there was a young lady who was a part of the crew that would antagonize me. She had a lot to say.

Now, we were smart because we were in our uniforms, so we knew we couldn't fight. However, we had a friend with us who was down for the cause and for $20 she took her down.

She walked right up to her and said, "They told me to punch you in face."

And BOOM! She punched her. They fought until we heard the police coming, then we scattered. We stole some of her items too. We didn't know that even with her doing the dirty work, we still would be found at fault. Yep, you guessed it. She pressed charges, and my best friend and I were included. This was during the summer before we left for college. Thankfully I paid close attention during the case.

I lost against the crew from across the street, so I knew how win mine. When I pressed my charges against the ones who had attacked me prior, I didn't realize that I needed a lawyer to speak for me and organize my case. There was more to the court of law than just my case versus theirs. There was not enough evidence to place me at the scene. I found doubt in her case against me and a second chance with God. Unfortunately, my friends didn't. This was two days before we left for college. We were facing these charges.

Long story short, I took my lawyer in the hallways and told him what I observed, and he WON my case. Two days later I was off to NC to North Carolina Central University. Looking back, it wasn't really a win, it was a bad seed planted in my future that was sure to show up. And boy did it.

Good Girl, Gone Bad, Gone Holy

During my sophomore year in college, my mommy found a church in Burlington. And on April 1, 2007, I was baptized. I was saved. I would travel faithfully to church in Burlington, sung in the choir, get the word, and everything else I could attend with what time I had. I was on fire for the Lord. Or so I thought.

Back then, I thought showing up, having an emotional experience and leaving meant I was changed. I would leave church, light my blunt and start planning for a night of partying. I needed more direction in this walk. Was I really ready for my transformation? Not even close.

Now there were great seeds planted, but I wasn't being disciplined or delivered.

My pastor at the time was amazing though. He was always giving me advice, and I could call on him for anything. I was so used to always having him to turn to. He was almost like a dad which was what I really needed: a male figure who could love me and guide me.

I remember getting into a fight after being at the club with a friend. Yes, a friend. That's what Hennessey and Hypnotic will do to you. We fought in the parking lot. Why were we mad? I remember it being because I spoke to someone she didn't like or something silly like that. Because she rode with me, her coat was in my car. After the fight, I was so mad I set her jacket on fire in front of her door at her apartment... her *campus apartment.*

What a crazy, drunken poor decision. I almost got expelled, but thankfully my pastor came to my meeting. Thank God someone in there knew him. God spared me.

My pastor had to eventually leave to his new church, and I don't blame him at all for leaving. God had him on assignment elsewhere, but for me that's when the chapter of my life went from getting better to bad. I was lost spiritually and didn't know at the time how to stay connected to God without church. I wasn't taught to study and spend time with Him. **With my pastor now gone, I didn't want to stay at the church.**

I would talk to God. I was well aware who He was, but I lost my true connection, or at least what I thought connected me. It seemed like a snowball effect of changes occurred. I was living in a one bedroom apartment with my then boyfriend who ended up leaving me, and then life got real. This was the same boyfriend for whom I used to drive drugs up and down the highway, package packs, pop pills, and drink. I thought we were like Bonnie and Clyde. I loved him, and thought he loved me. But life will show you who a person really is.

When they broke into his old house, I got the apartment for both of us. But he left. If I had to guess, it was pride. I came home one day and all of the furniture he gave me was gone! I had just finished working my tail off at a restaurant where I waited tables and bartended.

I guess I deserved it, if I look at it from his perspective. We had been then through somethings. It was after we went to the club one Sunday evening. After loads of alcohol there was an incident where a guy said something that pissed off my boyfriend. When we got in the car, I was still talking about the incident. He decided it was a good idea to mush me in the face. I decided to punch him the mouth and chipped his tooth. There I was, my hand bleeding and his tooth chipped.

Needless to say, it was long ride home. He didn't hit me back though. We argued through the rest of that night, and he got his tooth fixed the next day. It got really real when they started cutting off lights and water. I had to grow up and make decisions. I had to take on more jobs. I waited tables and bartended everywhere. I made pretty good money, worked long hours, but that's all my life became: work, work, work!

When I did have time, I began hanging out with friends who were just as lost as I was, drinking, smoking weed, or X-pills all to cloud my reality of life. I was all dressed up on the outside and broken to pieces on the inside. I made it look really good, but the Lord knew I wasn't happy.

Watching your friends graduate from college is rough. I attended all their ceremonies, each time holding back my tears because in my mind that should've been me. Getting to your senior year and having to drop out is hard. I was cheerleader too and missed out on Senior nights, awards, and everything I had worked so hard for.

This kind of setback makes you question yourself and say, *Was I not good enough? Smart enough?*

It wasn't any of that at all. God was still in control. He was teaching me a different lesson that college would never teach me. I was in "Rely on God 101."

Good Girl, Gone Bad, Gone Holy

As if things couldn't have gotten worse, they escalated. One drunken night with a so-called friend I was encouraged to commit the biggest mistake of my life. We went to a strip club and a young lady left her wallet.

My friend said, "Take the wallet, go buy some food, and we can cookout the next day."

I was *wasted!* I ended up at the store and used her card but signed my name in my drunken stupor. As I look back, all I can do is shake my head. I was at a popular store that had cameras. The cops came to get me the very next day. The young lady's dad turned out to be the sheriff. I remember the cops coming to my door, and I snuck out of my apartment and went to my friend who stayed in the same complex. I needed to plan for the crime I had committed.

Where was the money coming from to bail me out?

Who knew a bondman?

Would I be able to make a call?

After talking to my then best friend, we had a plan: call my ex because he had the money and connections to get me released the same night.

I remember sitting in the holding cell terrified and mad at myself. "Jennifer what were you thinking? God if you get me out of this!"

Thankfully my ex made some calls, paid the money, and got me out. Now I was facing felony charges and a long road to freedom. I was arrested at least two more times for failure to appear. When you hire janky lawyers, they don't always stay on top of your case, and as for me, I knew nothing of the court system. You miss court, they reschedule it. But I didn't know they issued a warrant for arrest as well.

Each time I sat in that holding cell I would say how I wouldn't do this again. I say each time because I ended up in that room a few more times. Some for failure to appear and one time for disturbing the peace.

I was able to get the felony charges dropped down to misdemeanors, and I was put on probation for a year. I was terminated unsuccessfully only because of traffic tickets. When you are on probation even a traffic ticket is a violation. I was getting those like candy as I was driving while my license was revoked.

I ended up being way over the time I was put on probation, so my lawyer and probation officer let the judge know outside of these traffic tickets I was good. I had followed all the directions of the probation order and paid my money. The judge let me off unsuccessfully, but either way it meant I was FREE!

Good Girl, Gone Bad, Gone Holy

Chapter 4. Power of your Words

I would be driving around in my squeaky '95 Ford truck, and I had to use an adapter to plug my boom box in because I didn't have a radio. Ghetto, but I was rolling, and it was mine). Now let me tell you why I had this hoopty. I had a Nissan *Sentra* prior to this car but it was repossessed. This was the first time I was paying a car note. Unfortunately, the car was repoed. It was a Wednesday and I was on my way to work. I walked outside to see my car being pulled away on a tow truck.

I luckily was able to stop him and get my belongings out of the car before he pulled away from my apartment.

I didn't have time to stress. I needed to get to work. I had bills to pay. My friend gave me a ride, and I worried about wheels later. My ex found me another car at the time, and it was only $1500. Thankfully my complex owed me $1500, and they cut the check for my referrals. I got my hoopty and all was well. I was just happy to have a car.

I remember many days riding in my truck listening to Gospel music, crying, praying, but MOST importantly believing for a breakthrough. MY faith back then was limitless. I trust God for the unthinkable simply because He never left me hanging. I would sing songs full of prophetic declaration over my life and I didn't even know it. God used music to force me to speak my destiny into existence. It was in the dark season that God used music to keep my hope and faith alive. Most people turn from God in turmoil.

Good Girl, Gone Bad, Gone Holy

Turmoil made me turn to Him. I figured if He could part the sea, He could save me. I was lost; lost friends, lost money, lost my car, lost my freedom. I had seen the court house more than any other house. I never gave up though, no matter how bad it got. I pressed forward. I took many steps back but doubled the amount I took forward.

I met a friend (now best friend) who in the mist of my transition gave me peace about my situation with my "friends." She said I could do more being quiet than I ever could opening my mouth. Juju with the Mouth was silenced.

The same friend invited me to her church. I told her I was looking for a new church-home and had no hope. I found a home at that very church of hers a year later. It took me an entire year to commit to this church. I needed to be sure it was where God wanted me to be, and well, I had trust issues. I began to get my focus back day by day, step by step. I was still lost, but I was finding my way. My faith was stronger than ever and even when things got worse I was confident that one day it would all work out for the better. I decided to take my life back and go to school. I applied and got accepted to Miller Motte College where I studied medical clinical assistance. They didn't welcome me at first with open arms due to my record, but my second recruiter assured me I could do whatever I put my mind to. I attended and graduated with honors. I even got accepted to work at my internship. What made this so special was that I was told I would never get the internship or the job. Not only did he hire me at this practice, but I was the FIRST ever hired.

God showed me the power of faith talk and I followed my faith with actions. I didn't know what the end would look like, but I trusted it would be miraculous. I knew God would change the rules for me simply because I trusted Him. I went into territory that told me no and let God give me a YES!

What you speak out your mouth is powerful. The power of life and death are in the tongue.

(Proverbs 18:21).

As a man thinkith in his heart so he is.

(Proverbs 23:7).

Often times what Is holding us back from moving forward is the words coming out of our mouths. You can speak yourself into a blessing or into a curse. Choose your words wisely.

Chapter 5. The Unthinkable Leave the First Time

"I loved you, you were it for me. I was really going to marry you."

Those words brought me peace as I sat across from the man I once loved with all my being. We had run into each other after several years had passed, and he wanted to "talk." I agreed. He and I tried to be friends, but I'm sure you wouldn't believe me if I told you: he used to physically abuse me.

Let's rewind.

I met this ex-boyfriend at a bar I used to frequent. He had spoken to me a few times before and would even buy my girls and I some drinks. He was my dream guy. For years, I had been searching to fill the void created when my dad wasn't there for me. This boyfriend gave the security, love, and provision I always needed. thought those things found in someone else would replace the void I had in my life.

Domestic violence isn't something you plan for. You don't plan for a violent and aggressive member of your home, a home that is built on love. Aggression and violence is the antithesis of love, or maybe even it is the misdirection of it. You don't expect

this. It's often confused as love because typically after the man/woman abuse you they love you afterwards, apologizing about how they will never do it again. The love tries to cover the pain and clouds your reality of what just happened. You start to believe
it won't happen it again because they "love" you.

I was shocked. This couldn't be coming from the man I love, make love to, travel with, laugh with, share dreams with. No one ever expects to be a victim of domestic violence. Matter of fact I was one of those, *that won't happen to me*, kind of woman. I just knew I would kick whoever's behind and keep it moving if they ever tried. I was a fighter back then. But this was a grown six foot, about one hundred and eight five pounds of bench pressing man. He has more strength than I ever had. Trying to go blow for blow was impossible. With each blow, I was the one knocked down.
I was practically staying with him, and didn't have want for anything. He provided me with literally anything I asked for or even voiced as a need.

My dating views were different then. I wanted the bad boy with a lot of money, full of adventure, and could give me a flat out good time. I dated guys that made me feel good, that made me feel emotionally and financially secure. If he drove a nice car, had his own place, and had decent head on his shoulders, I was game. I didn't care about how he fed my spirit or mind. I was more concerned about my fleshly desires and he cured them.

We did everything together and had so much fun! I was madly in love with this man for more reasons than I could remember. We just clicked in that season of my life.

He cooked for me. I remember the first meal he made me, they were enchiladas. We actually kind of made them together, but he wanted to do something special for me. He let me watch for the majority of the time while he cooked and I drank. Grey Goose and cranberry was our drink of choice. When the food was done, we ate on the couch watching TV. Nothing fancy, simplicity was our thing. My feet across his lap, his plate on my legs and mine on my lap, drinks in hand. That was the typical "us."

He showered me with gifts. We had the kind of love that just felt right. He would cater to my every need. He would come by a lot of nights and just sit on my balcony and smoke cigs, drink, and talk to me about my life and past pains.

I felt EXREMELY safe with him. He carried a gun and was thoroughly respected by his peers. He was the leader. I always felt safe with him until *that* night.

It was the kind of love you think you've always wanted. Looking back, I was settling for my fleshly desires and short term healing for my daddy wounds.

We took trips, ate at fine restaurants, but the majority of our relationship was sex, alcohol, and good times. He wouldn't tell me, but I knew he sold drugs. I saw them in the house, but then again most of my former boyfriends all dealt drugs. It didn't bother me. I should have run for the hills. I've seen what happens to the girlfriend of drug dealers. I know a few ladies personally who have done time in prison because of their men.

I decided that he kept his drug dealing a secret to "keep me safe."

He also had a porn company at the time. He actually told me about this business. I was into porn back then so it didn't bother me at all. I actually wanted to view a taping. He was renting the home next door, which is where they would tape. He would never let me go over there though. I guess this was his way of protecting me or he was hiding something from me. He may have even been one of the participants.

I went to church even in the midst of this toxic relationship, but when you aren't being fed real scriptural food, you take the appetizer and run. At the time, I would show up, read the scripture and my Bible didn't see me again until the following week. I was preached into an emotionally happy place that would get me through the week until I showed up again. I needed the second course. I needed the meat of God's word. I needed to be taught what it meant to live the word and not just hear it.

I got too comfortable with him. I started to believe what I wanted and do what I wanted. We were basically living together, and he would give me cash every day that I was running low on cash. One day I went into his stash and took some cash without asking.

Dead wrong. I didn't think he would notice. Dealing with drug dealers as former boyfriends, most of my dating career money was just expendable, and they never noticed. They never told me to just take what I needed. I figured that was the case with this relationship. But he was *livid*!

I tried to explain, but he wasn't having it, and he immediately put me out. I mean I had my own place, but I always stayed at his house. I cried. I begged, and I pleaded, but he felt betrayed— rightfully so. The pain was horrible. How could I blame him? His "baby girl" as he so lovingly called me had stolen from him. If you know anything about street dudes, they don't that lightly. They would kill someone for this type of behavior.

I remember him saying in the midst of yelling, "Nah man, not my baby girl." I had done the unthinkable to him.

I remember listening to Keri Hilson's song, "Tell Him the Truth" over and over again. He was such a consistent part of my life, and after this everything changed. I became familiar with our routine. Breaking this routine made the pain even more apparent. When you are used to waking up to someone daily, checking in, and sleeping every night you regret ever hurting them just to go back to how things were. Enjoying a consistent routine with the wrong man only leads to wanting the same consistent routine with yet another man who isn't good for you.

We remained friends after the break up. We shared a few of the same friends and hung out at some of the same spots so naturally we ran into each other often. This of course created the ping-pong, back and forth.

"We are not together but we still kick it" stage.

In this stage, you are still going through the motions but lacking the commitment piece. Still sleeping together, occasional dates, but nothing was consistent. This hurt me bad, but I was so desperate to show him that I had changed so I settled for whatever time I could get from him.

Now throughout our relationship I had a feeling that my ex was seeing other women. I had a little proof, but was so high in love that was blinded. But all things come to light. Back then I called it intuition, but I now know it to be Holy Spirit who was leading and guiding me into truth.

After months of going back and forth, him lying to me, catching him with other women, and the list goes on. I saw him out at a local strip club He would go there often so it was to no surprise he was there. He had always had huge problem with drinking and would drink until he vomited blood when we were together and of course on this night he was *drunk*. I was concerned back then, and would often voice my opinion on his alcohol intake.

I did not drive this particular evening, and his uncle asked me to drive him home. My ex was already trying to come on to me and was getting on my nerves. He was grabbing me, expressing his love, trying to "work it out", buy me drinks his normal routine when saw me out.

My gut told me NO don't do it! Don't drive him home, let his uncle Go home, and he will be just fine. Then my heartstrings started playing a tune that was all too familiar. I began to think, "*If I don't get him home safely he may crash.* Being myself and still loving him, I said I would take him home. We got in the van, and I am taking him home to drop him off he had always had more than one car so he wouldn't be stranded in the morning. I could drop him off, drive his car to my place and he could arrange to get it the next day. I get to his house and he decides he wants me to stay.

This was typical, but tonight I wasn't having it. I was going home and said, "No, I'll just take you home," is what he said.

Now to me he seemed to have sobered up a little, so I said ok. Plus, we didn't stay far from each other. We got to my apartment complex and all hell breaks! He had to drive me home because I caught a ride to the strip club. So, we left and arrived at my apartment complex. I didn't want to stay at his house. We sat in the car and talked for a matter of minutes. I was upset because I felt like all he wanted was sex. If he wanted me, he needed to commit, and before I could blink, I was being snatched out of the car by the collar of my shirt, dragged to the ground, fought back, and things got worse. I swung, and so did he. I was punched in the head multiple times, thrown to the ground, kicked, and stomped. While on the ground, I tried to call 911, but my phone was snatched and thrown across the parking lot. I rolled myself into a ball for protection, when he finally came to and stopped. I ran inside of my home and collapsed on the floor and just cried. He came in after and tried to apologize. I just screamed and told him to get away from me.

I was calling the cops!

Once I calmed down I went for my phone, which was shattered so I couldn't call anyone. Luckily, I had friends who stayed in my complex, and I went to their apartment. My home girl answered her door and was shocked, scared, and let me use her phone to call the police. They came with the ambulance. She kept asking me what happened, and I could not speak. I just cried.

They took one look at me and said, "your face and head are swollen. You could be having some bleeding on your brain."

I was terrified and went to the hospital. The police got his information and went to pick him up. Riding alone in that ambulance did something to me.

I made it to the hospital and had yet to tell someone what was happening. Luckily my mother, a nurse, had her number in a database. Since my phone was shattered I had no way of reaching anyone. She and her now husband we very angry to say the least and wanted to come yoke him up. I declined and said no I'll be fine. Instead of letting him get what he deserved, I decided not to physically retaliate. They ran test, gave me meds and I caught a cab home. Thankfully they didn't find anything in my test to be scared of. I had bruises everywhere, swollen face and scratches but otherwise I was ok and most importantly alive.

I VOWED right there this wasn't happening again, and I would do everything in my power to make sure no young woman went without hearing this story.

Chapter 6. The Days After

The aftermath of domestic violence can be more horrifying than the incident. Emotionally I was confused. I felt lost, abandoned. rejected, I was confused because I knew the emotional pain of love but the physical was different.

I finally knew what it meant to love someone who has put his or her hands on you. It's the weirdest thing ever. You yearn for this person because you feel like you love them, but common sense says NO! You still want to feel their embrace but you know you have to leave them alone. It's hard, I can't even lie to you. My emotions were EVERYWHERE! So, I did what I had to in the days moving forward. You need to leave them alone for your safety, and sanity.

Love is, according to 1 Corinthians 13:4-10 The Message (MSG)

> *If I give everything I own to the poor and even go to the stake to be burned as a martyr, but I don't love, I've gotten nowhere. So, no matter what I say, what I believe, and what I do, I'm bankrupt without love.*

> *Love never gives up.*
> *Love cares more for others than for self.*
> *Love doesn't want what it doesn't have.*
> *Love doesn't strut,*
> *Doesn't have a swelled head,*
> *Doesn't force itself on others,*

Isn't always "me first,"
Doesn't fly off the handle,
Doesn't keep score of the sins of others,
Doesn't revel when others grovel,
Takes pleasure in the flowering of truth,
Puts up with anything,
Trusts God always,
Always looks for the best,
Never looks back,
But keeps going to the end.

What he and I had wasn't love. It was lust.

I had to get a restraining order and everything. You go to the courthouse and tell the story over and over you. You *relive* the entire event. It was so hard to go through. You don't want to keep telling the story or reliving the events. It's like going through emotional HELL! I cried a lot that day. I was depressed! Thankfully through this ordeal I didn't have to see his face. That would've made it even hard. Telling this story now brings me even more healing. I happy I got away.

As if I hadn't been through enough, I got a phone call a few days later...FROM HIS WIFE! Talk about pissed, sad, hurt, confused, and mad all over again. I relived the event again, telling her the sickening and heartbreaking story. I gave her the truth she so desperately sought. I forget what she said but most importantly she informed me this wasn't the first time. She was calm, very respectful, and I could tell her heart went out to me. I didn't apologize to her. She said she was sorry I had to go through this. I don't know how this hurt him or anyone else at the time/ I had detached myself. It was a bad situation from my poor choices.

Going to court became a headache, and I had already had my share of court dates that I could stomach. To be honest with you I went to every court date but the last one. I know some may think it is crazy, but I woke up and felt I didn't need to go.

I told God He could handle it. I did not want to see the court room or my ex. I knew there would be a deeper punishment. You literally reap what you sow. I had medical bills and all, but I just didn't go. I was over it and handed it completely over to God. As for the protective order, he did break the guidelines of the order a few times but it never went too far. The judge was made aware and reinforced days. I didn't have to come to court prior to the last date. I was just done. I didn't have to deal with him hurting me anymore.

I was able to take away a lot from this ordeal and hopefully it helps you for the future. Pay attention to your partner's habits. My ex had a bad drinking habit, and although he never acted like this before, he had it in him. He had an anger streak I could see early on. He would get really angry about situations that had nothing to do with me, but it was an EXTREME anger. LEAVE THE FIRST TIME! It's easier said than done, but let me be a living example of what it looks like. You can leave, disconnect and move on with life even through the pain.

You don't want to lose your life because
you "loved them."

TELL SOMEONE! So many suffer in silence.
Tell someone or people you can trust and who will
protect you from you. Your vision is cloudy in these
situations, and you need someone who can see for
you! Communicating what's happening will start
providing a way of escape.

Pray for God to protect you, heal you, and set
you free. You don't want this to be something that
keeps you spiritually bound. Break the soul tie and the
root of this attack and live free. Seek the lord like
never before and stay soaked in prayer. Here is an
example of a prayer you can pray.

*Father in Jesus precious name I asked
that you untie me from every relationship
that wasn't approved by you. Any
relationship that came to physically,
emotionally, or spiritually harm me. Any and
all relationship based on lust. Cover me,
release me, and heal me. amen*

FORGIVE THEM. It is not for them it is
for YOU. Years after the ordeal, I actually saw my ex
again and still do from time to time. I forgave him,
moved on with my life, and though we aren't friends
when we see each other, there isn't any bad
blood. Recently he even apologized, commended me
on moving forward and being successful in life. I am
free from hatred and bitterness, because I let God show
me how to forgive him. I allowed myself to be in his

34

shoes before God. I allowed God to let me see him the way He did. God didn't Hate him and He didn't love him less. I adapted God's compassion and forgave him.

But if you do not forgive others their trespasses, neither will your Father forgive your trespasses.

Matthew 6:15 ESV

And whenever you stand praying, forgive, if you have anything against anyone, so that your Father also who is in heaven may forgive you your trespasses."

Mark 11:25 ESV

Do yourself a favor: stay free. Even though I didn't go to the last court date, we all really do end up going anyways. God is going to judge and hold us accountable for our time spent on earth. He is keeping a good record of the things we haven't repented for.

Good Girl, Gone Bad, Gone Holy

Chapter 7. Ask God for Another Chance

Bad decisions have a domino effect. I had pretty much tarnished my name, credibility, and image. Now at this point in my life I knew God. I always have known Him. But I wasn't TRUE to Him. My loyalty was elsewhere. I was so broken and lost that I had to really think? What the heck do I do now?

I had to contact lawyers because I was at one time facing felony charges. I remember my two abortions, I remember selling drugs, driving drugs, and taking drugs. I remember weighing the weed, bagging it all while smoking it. I remember taking the e-pills and selling them behind the bar to customers and co-workers. I remember getting drunk and knocking the power out on my street, wrecking my sister's car.

I remember having sex without protection, dating married men (knowingly and unknowingly). I remember even considering selling my body for sex because my record stopped me from getting a job. I remember talking trash behind peoples' backs, fighting out of fear, and stealing from malls. I remember the conversation when I was going to sell my body for money:

"You will just meet them at the hotel I tell you, and you will receive the money before you go in. Just be nice, it's just a good time, and then you leave, paid."

I am reminded from what God saved me. When you get to a low place and have nothing you can do to survive, it's not Mommy and Daddy who could rescue me. It was me and Jesus. I had no other source. You ask God for another chance! God will use situations to wake you up! He is truly jealous for us. God wants our attention, and when He doesn't get it willingly, He will intervene and almost force us. At this point, I thought to God, *I am a hot mess and I NEED YOU! Fix me first, though.*

Why me first? Because I was the root of my issues. There was change that needed to happen in me first. God showed me that He had great things for me, but I wasn't going to get them with an empty, ugly, deceitful heart. I had to change. Change isn't comfortable.

When you see people around you enjoying life full of everything you too enjoy but God says you can't have whew! ITS HARD TO JUST SAY NO! Even now I have to be careful what environments I put myself in as I am still being delivered. My walk isn't perfect but daily God graces me to start over and repent. And each and every time he wraps me in his loving presence and welcomes me. With God, there isn't any rejection. He always says, "Yes my daughter come to me for I have longed to spend time with you."

I love God not because someone told me too. I love him because he first loved me and pursued me relentlessly. How could you not serve Him, how could you not surrender your will? He was loyal to me when I wasn't even loyal to myself.

So, what did I do? One day in May, 2012, I sat with a good friend of mine who shared her journey with Christ. Her story inspired me to surrender fully to God mind, body, and spirit. She mentioned to me how abstaining from sex had played a major role in her transformation. I had played the fence long enough anyway so what did I have to lose. She looked at me with a straight face and said "You know you have to give up bartending too, right?"

Now, that was my bread and butter. How could I quit doing that? I needed and depended on that income to survive. Remember, I had no rich parents taking care of me. It was just me. So, I prayed for God to replace that income all summer long. I would go to word feeling convicted for even being there. I was so torn in my spirit. How could I be a bartender serving spirits and I am called to cast them out!

Woe to those who are heroes at drinking wine and champions at mixing drinks.

Isiah 5:22 NIV

In September of 2012, that same good friend told me about a multilevel marketing company. She shared their amazing products with me. She tried the products, and after one conversation with the woman who she purchased from, I was sold. I knew I could market this product and be successful with this business. It made sense to me: wellness, beauty, women. Sign me up!

September 9, 2012 changed my life forever. I began sharing this wonderful product and opportunity to everyone I knew and even strangers. The business had replaced the income from bartending, and in November I stopped bartending. Halleluiah!

I met my fiancé as well in November.

Funny how when you trust God and let go of what He doesn't have for you, you have the room for what He does. I was almost free. I still was at my other job, which I hated so badly, but was grateful they took me on flaws, record, and all. I got engaged on March 9th, and finally I was able to quit my job and work my business from home on March 29, 2013.

Now I never thought after 7 months of starting my business I'd make more money than I'd ever imagine and be so secure. I never knew in May 2012 when I surrender my heart and body to God that He would send my now soon to be husband and change my life completely around.

Had I not went to lunch with my sister-friend that warm day in May, I wouldn't have been inspired to take the next step in my transformation. I didn't change immediately, but that day I made major decision. I didn't look back.

I asked God for another chance. Not just because of this situation but everything leading up to it and what will come after. You see I am tired of chasing the crowd and doing things my way and failing. I didn't want the reality of a felony record and never being able to get ahead to be my portion in life. I knew better than to think that's all God had for me. So, he softened my heart, opened my mind, and led me to a place of pure repentance.

"Lord, fix me."

God change me first and this is still my prayer. Less of me and more of You. Show me what it's like to be like You, made in your image. Show me what that looks like, show me what my heart should look like, what my mind should think about, what my speech should sound like and what my purpose looked like.

I didn't start looking at anything else other than me and what I needed to fix me. I prayed day in and day out. As I prayed and worked towards being a better me God starting shaping me and still is. He started testing me too. He would allow certain situation to occur to see if I learned my lesson.

One thing I had to learn for sure was where my security came from, and that was God. I could seek all these earthly "treasures," but they would never amount to the peace, love, and joy God could give me.

Look deep inside and see what needs to change. Ask God for another shot at your destiny. He's definitely waiting for you and has all the love and encouragement you need to get it right. TRUST HIM!

Good Girl, Gone Bad, Gone Holy

Chapter 8. The Aisle I Never Walked

He walked into church one Sunday, and a few Sundays later we exchanged words, laughs, and then numbers on November 4th 2012. I was one of the leaders of the singles ministries at my church and we all gathered after service one day. We had a second service and were deciding if we were coming back. I asked him, and he said he was. We talked for the rest of the day, literally even through service. The days following, we instantly clicked.

I discussed where I was in my life with him. I was surrendered to God, on fire for God, and let my standards be known from day one that I was preparing for my one day husband. This was new to him, but he himself was on a path to get closer to God, so he went with it. And well, I guess you can say, he liked me a little. We went on a few amazing dates and quickly fell in love. Our dates were never boring and we would randomly go bowling or play pool.

It was December 21st 2012 when he asked me into courtship. We had gone on a date to a "wine and design." He asked me that evening in the car to marry him, and I accepted. He kept saying "olive juice" repeatedly. I did not understand and eventually caught on. He was saying, "I love you." We were dating with purpose, and we saw things going towards marriage. We began to explore the idea.

He was really good friends with my pastor, and this gave me ease. This was the same church and pastor that restored and built my faith in God. I had been attending for 2 years at the time. My fiancé was a co-worker of my pastor, and he never knew my pastor was in fact a pastor until he asked about going to church. Then my Pastor invited him to church where we met. My fiancé was the new kid in town at church, and because there weren't that many young adults, he didn't go unnoticed. Plus, he was handsome.

My fiancé planned a trip to the beach in March. This was some time for us to get away, and he could meet my grandparents. I packed and got ready. I was excited, I pretty much knew this would be the proposal weekend even though he tried to throw me off, saying something about the ring not being ready. I loved him and any moment I was able to spend with him made me happy, so I didn't care either way. By this time, I was sure we would be together for the rest of our lives, what's the rush, right?

He was nervous and excited from what I can I remember.

On March 9, 2013 while walking on the beach We began talking about a number of things. Life, love, our future, and we people watched. We walked a little while longer, and while getting ready to take a picture he proposed to me the only words from the proposal I could remember, as he got down on his knee. He said I made him a better man and better son. That is all he said, and I said yes. This was the happiest day of my life and one I'll never forget. We were so in sync that we actually wore the same outfit, totally unplanned, but to me this was a sign from heaven that today was the perfect day, and we were meant for each other.

I helped him launch two businesses and a blog, and I no longer had a need to work my own business at 26. We would spend every weekend together. We would cry on Sundays when we split, and then be back on the phone in minutes as he drove back home to Charlotte, North Carolina. I remember the first time I made a $9,0000 check in my business in one month, and we looked at each other and decided we would go shopping. We literally went on a shopping spree that day spent about $500 a piece but that's good shopping when you NEVER could drop that kind of money in one setting. What I loved about him was that we never had to do anything fancy to have fun. We could stay at home and laugh at the same online videos over and over, sing songs like we were having our own private concert, and wouldn't have a care in the world. It was a fast-paced ride that came to an abrupt end, just like a roller coaster.

In July things began to get a little rocky, disagreements began to surface, and bickering became normal. People may consider this normal couple stuff, right? Well that wasn't normal for us. We normally just got along, but now the work had to be done. This was the test of whether or not would be able to weather a storm or in this case an argument. One major key to a healthy lasting relationship is communication. Now we had to see if we could effectively communicate and work through this.

I remember an argument that occurred because I lovingly said that my mother showed up. Years later I can honestly state that I said some hurtful things to him. I said things like: "You're supposed to love me like the church. That means you put me first, but you don't understand what that means" or

"Stay there I'll be fine. I don't need you anyway."

I was pissed he didn't come to a traffic court date with me because he wanted to watch a popular trial on TV. He knew my license was already revoked so I thought he would have at least drove me. I was trying to adopt this "moving as a unit" idea so I wanted him to go everywhere I went. In my eyes, he was dead wrong. I made sure he knew I felt that way by speaking down on him and in my opinion selfish judgement.

We had been together for seven months by this time. When we were riding in the car, I heard clearly in my spirit "this is too much for him". We had just come back from bailing my sister out of jail. He told me that sometimes he felt like he wasn't good enough, and I forget his exact words but something was too much.

We were going away for business one weekend, and it was like God shook me and said this is too much for my fiancé. Something just was not right. He told me some things that were on his heart one week prior to us breaking up.

By the end of the weekend we were sure we wanted to be married and move forward. He even grabbed my hand at dinner one night while we were away and said after what he had learned from other husbands, he knew there was something he could do better, and he was more than sure he wanted to spend the rest of his life with me.

That Monday after we came back from St. Louis, he stepped outside to speak to his mom for three hours, and y'all already know that made me super suspect and resulted in yet another argument. In the midst of us arguing, God told me to shut up and to ask him to pray with me.

He told me NO! Shook me to the core. The man I loved so much was so mad he couldn't even pray with me, but proclaimed with God we could get through anything? God where are you, I need You to step in. I called my Pastor to let him know what was going on and thankfully he talked to him and calmed him down. So I thought.

My then fiancé came to my home and told me he was going home to spend time with his mom, and he would see me Friday. He text messaged me to tell me he loved me and basically everything would be ok.

I come home Wednesday and he had taken all his things from my apartment and left my key.

I was devastated and sent a text saying, "I'm not mad but what happened."

No response.

I later received an email from my then fiancé breaking up with me. Yes, an email. After all we built together and were working towards, I got an email.

You're probably wondering what happen after the email. I did what most girls do: call their mommy. I called, I wept and wept crying out, "what did I do. Why wont he talk to me?!"

Of course, I tried to talk to him, if not to work it out to get closure. I wasn't successful. We set a date two weeks later, and then he removed himself from all contact with me.

Can you imagine? One week everything being amazing, sending out your wedding invitations, cake tasting,1st dance song, flower girl dress, bride maids' shoes, picked up your wedding dress, picked out flowers, and then the next week in complete misery? That had become my life.

We spoke in maybe two emails about canceling the wedding, which I was left to do basically by myself. He wouldn't even answer the phone to discuss that. Email was all I worth after all of this. Every day was rough. I didn't wake up one day without a tear in my eye and an ache in my heart. Friends tried to connect us, family, and nothing worked he was set in his mind. I had to get used to my "new normal" without him. Every move I made reminded me of him because I didn't make a move without him in mind.

The pain got so deep I had to be put on anti-depressants just to keep from crying. There were so many days I just wanted to stop crying. My life was wake up pop a pill, midday pop a pill, go to bed pop a pill. For a good 30 days that pill was going to control me.

I met with my mother weekly for lunch. She wanted to be sure I'd have enough strength for the next week. You will need your mother's love. I became dependent on the relief. Thoughts of not being good enough, never being married, I'm not pretty enough, he may come back, my past will always stop me, just pray and God will fix it, let it go, hold on. My mind was always running.

People would ask me how I was doing, and I couldn't even lie. I was broken, and it was all over my face. My smile wasn't even the same. My heart was broken and my best friend, my roll dog, business partner, my love, my heart, my babe, my inside jokester and then fiancé—that was also gone. To add insult to injury he mailed me my wedding band.

How was I?

Hurt to the core, the worst pain I've ever felt in my life, but I kept going in the midst of each tear. I was in the middle of an internship for school and still went and completed my hours. Everywhere I went there was someone getting married or engaged which broke me every time. I went to Miami to get away after the ordeal and went to get my nails done. There was a bridal shower going on!

I had a business to run that thankfully my leaders stepped right in and took over for me. I experienced many weak days, long mornings and nights. No sleep, couldn't eat. You know how that goes. There was no closure. Just an end. And I had to deal with it.

How do you move forward from this?

God's grace, love, strength, and comfort. Thank God for His grace! I promise if I didn't know Jesus I'd been lost with no direction. He kept my mind, wiped my tears and is healing my heart. I put my confidence solely in HIM and he gave me the courage to endure. Are there days I still cry? Yes, but each day is better than the day before. Have I seen him or spoke to him since? No. I haven't seen him or spoken to him. Sometimes you have to just accept the apology you will never get and close chapters without real closure and just flat out TRUST GOD!

God will bless me with a man who will fight for us to work, accept every bit of my testimony, and love me like Christ loved the church. I have no doubts in that. I am glad to know that He saved me from the wrong guy.

It said a lot. Some things I could agree with, and some will probably never be discussed.

He wrote in a way that was formal, like it was business. He wrote how he felt I was not being open or honest, accountable, or endearing. He said he felt "vulnerable." He wrote how I made time for others, valued my own time, but not his nor his presence. He said that he had to compete for my time, and that event meant competing against time when I was making money. What hurt him was that I would not make amends with his mother, that he asked me to do it for him, and I told him we must "agree to disagree." It was clear in his eyes that I was a stubborn person, selfish, and demanding. We had tried to put in for a townhouse, and he brought this up in the email, saying their rejection because of my background was enough to show him a record of my past. And that is where he says he began to "connect the dots." He felt I was always hiding something, that I was misleading him, and that I was not open about my history.

One reason he felt the need to leave was my past mistakes. Although yes, I did tell him on paper I didn't look great. He told me he wanted to know me for me, and I believed this. But I should've went into detail.

Though I see a lot of where he was coming from, he was still in error. We both were. He was in error because he was aware of my past. I did in fact tell him. When he saw it on paper in legal terms it scared him. He also didn't handle the split in an honorable fashion. He not only broke up with me via email but would communicate on small issues like canceling caterers using email as if I was just some business acquaintance. He was hard to communicate with even when I was being reasonable and accepted his decision. I may be wrong, but when you are going to marry someone you should be able to communicate. He just ran and sent an email, and I never heard from him again. It's deception when you tell someone on a Saturday you love them and can't wait to marry them, and then Monday you leave saying we will talk Friday, and you vanish on a Wednesday. In one week, my life had been forever altered—and it seemed not to matter to him!

Since then I've seen VERY clear why we couldn't be together. I felt like God snatched him out of my heart, life and soul. He had to. I was going to fight for him. God knows how loyal I am. God had to deal with me instantly for me to really let go.

Your true partner in life, the right man for you, will see you for who you are TODAY and won't care but then there are those who will hold it against you be careful. I'm proud of my past it made me the amazing woman I am today. I wouldn't change any of it! It brought me to Jesus and part of why this book had to be wrote to share with you.

So, what did I learn?

I NEEDED work. I had no patience, I wasn't ready to submit. I was in a place in life where I thought I knew what being a wife was, and boy was I wrong. PRAY! Sisters and brothers pray long and hard and don't move until you hear God say, "Yes he/she is it!"

One thing I've learned in this season since the breakup was how to hear from God. You want to be able to truly hear God say he/she is one. You want to make sure their word adds up to their actions. My ex wrote many bogs on our relationship, God, and more but when it was time to put and I quote "with God we can make it through anything" to action there was no fruit. Some can speak it and not live it discern wisely.

KEEP GOD IN THE CENTER ALWAYS! It will take more than going to church together. Ladies, you want a husband who pushes you towards Christ daily, respects your purity 100%, prays with and for you, pursues you passionately, is your teammate, friend, provider, protector, and leader, then keep God at the center of your every action.

Don't fall in love with potential. Although my then fiancé was on his way to a better relationship with God, he wasn't ready for a relationship with me. God was in the molding process with me as well. Had I known now what I knew then, I would let our friendship grow before a relationship. He began growing spiritually and mentally, but I feel the relationship was in the way. He did things because of me and not because it was to please God. He needed to surrender to God's will for his life first. When that is done, the sacrifice for one another can take place. Sometimes you have to just shut up and think of the other person and not yourself. When you can, revisit the issue when you both can effectively communicate. Pick and choose your battles some just aren't worth it.

Communication is key: Figure out how your lady/man communicates. One thing I know now is that he would shut down a lot and I would push forward with whatever I wanted to talk about or deal with. Didn't work just pushed him further into his shell. He was not confrontational at all.

GO TO PREMARITAL COUNSELING! You need that 3rd voice of reason to help you along the way. You need wise counsel from someone who has already been through some of the good and bad things you will experience on your journey. If you see where you guys are headed start ASP. Marriage is a huge decision and you don't want to make the decision off emotions. Had we gone as much as needed we would've ended a little smoother than email?

Ladies, you can't make him lead you! Period. The man is the leader by his choice, and some guys just aren't ready. Trying to develop him into that will lead to a brick wall. Let God make a man out of him before you make a husband out of him.

Learn to submit first to God so you can submit to your one-day husband. I remember an argument my ex and I got into about him not coming to traffic court with me because he wanted to watch the Zimmerman trial. It ended ugly, and I called off the wedding and his mother felt disrespected. Did I disrespect her? He wanted me to apologize, and my pride wouldn't let me do it. I felt if I started apologizing about our issues now, I'd be apologizing forever. In marriage, sometimes you will have to do what's best for the both of you meaning killing your prideful flesh to please your mate and keep the peace. Especially if he is a "mama's boy," his mama will trump you. With that said, establish boundaries in your relationship when it comes to your parents. When you become one-flesh it's you and your partner. Not you him/her and their parents.

Don't go into business with your fiancé. Wait until you are sure they are the one. I helped my ex start an online store and built a business for/with him with my MLM business for which he still got a check. It used to grind my gears that he gets paid off of my efforts, but I trusted God. He sees and knows all. My goal was always to add to his life.

When it's over, REMAIN who you are. People can say what they want after a break up, but the truth in your life will speak highly for you. Don't retaliate out of anger, just hold your peace. I didn't know how much I had grown until this breakup. I didn't do things the angry emotions could have.

Chapter 9. Just Obey God for the Keys

I was leaving from lunch with my friends, it was raining, and I saw a homeless guy standing in the rain. I looked in my car to see what I had to give him (homeless people touch my heart, always have). So, I saw my umbrella, and God was like give it to him. I won't lie, I was reluctant. It was a good umbrella, but I said, 'Hey, I can get another. It's not that deep, you never how many storms that umbrella will cover him in.' So, I went on my way to Wal-Mart, and then couldn't find a spot close enough to the door. I circled around, and then said, 'Fine this park will do,' but then noticed another woman (closer parking) unloading and getting ready to leave. I could've went with the spot behind me or been patient and got the closer park. God said, 'Be patient,' so I waited. As she began to pull out another spot closer became open and another two spots along with hers. They all pulled out at the same time. Suddenly it is as if the entire parking lot became empty for me. When you are obedient to God, and patiently wait on Him, He won't only open the doors you desire but even better ones.

Have you ever asked God for something and then didn't get it in "your timing?" Have you considered that maybe you hadn't been obedient to what He has been asking of you? We all have different desires and needs we so desperately seek from God. A lot of times we get mad at God and wonder why He hasn't blessed us. We feel like our prayers aren't being heard, and that's not true. God sees, hears, and knows all, but He also requires a level of obedience in our lives. It's bigger than just showing up to church on Sunday. Anyone can do that. It's a heart issue. Is God living and dwelling in your heart? Are you spending time with him in devotion and worship? Are you feeding your mind, body, and soul Gods daily bread?

> And he said to him, "You shall love the Lord your God with all your heart and with all your soul and with all your mind. This is the great and first commandment. And a second is like it: You shall love your neighbor as yourself. On these two commandments depend all the Law and the Prophets."

> Matthew 22:37-40 ESV

God wants our whole hearts period! He also wants us to love our neighbors. So, with that said love people even when they wrong you love them anyway. When you disobey God, doesn't He still love you? YES! You woke up today didn't you? What if your next blessing is caught in how you bless someone who has wronged you? What if God is asking you to move to a new city? quit a job? Cut off a fruitless relationship or simply to just be still and know he is God?

Obedience not only opens doors, but it covers you for the future. Think about the woman with the empty jars. In the story, Elisha told the woman to ask her neighbors for empty jars. These were faith instructions. She needed to be obedient and do as He said in order for God to move on her behalf. She collected the jars and was then told to go home and close the door. Often times, God will perform His best miracles in the secret place. Think about your prayer time. Have you ever encountered God's presence so strongly that you left your prayer time completely changed? This is just like that. Now because she followed directions, her jars overflowed with oil. The oil could be used to pay off her debts, while leaving extra for her family.

Often times God is just looking for you to obey the simple instructions in order to receive the big blessings. Had she not obeyed and gathered all the empty jars she wouldn't have received her overflow. Now let's go deeper. Take Ruth, for instance. She obeyed and left to be with Naomi and her family in a strange land. Her obedience landed her the COVERING Boaz.

Obedience is the currency of the kingdom. There are things God has asked me to do to move forward. He asked me to stop smoking weed at one point, and well, when I was put on probation I had no choice but to quit.   He asked me to guard my tongue, obey my parents even when they were wrong, love my friends, pass their flaws because I HAD MY OWN! He told me to go back to school, apply for jobs, even when my record said, "Girl good luck at McDonalds.

God simply wanted me to TRUST him.

Chapter 10. Circumcise your Cycles

In my journey even since the broken engagement, I've found myself in a dating cycle I had to end. The cycle looked like this. You date someone, and the first 90 days or so are amazing. Then you see who "they" really are. You discover that you weren't really a good fit for each other, but you stay because of all the time you have spent and emotions you have invested. Some of us have even created a soul tie, and now you feel trapped in this emotional roller coaster. You guys are good one day and not the next. You are thinking let's give it another shot only for it to fail yet again and leave you more confused. Then you are left trying to figure out when you got to this place...frustrating, I know!

You know deep down inside you deserve better and what you have with this person isn't going anywhere. No commitments are being made, there's no purpose, and you have no peace about being with this person. It's purely your emotions that have you attached, and that's it! I've been here too many times, and watched friends and even people on social media go through this insane cycle.

I've come up with some effective steps to set you and the other person free!

Step 1: Identify the main reason why you need to spilt.

It can be a difference in life goals, lack of respect, no purpose, difference in religions, morals, values, whatever it is put a name to it so you are clear why it will not work. If you can't have a conversation with this person, you may need a mediator (voice of reason) to help you and that's ok. (Seek help as needed). Finding out why you keep going back and forth is the key to not repeating it in the future. Now this could be deeper. It could be because your mom did and now it passed down to you. Generationally these things can transfer spiritually. You will need to come to a middle ground on why this isn't right for either of you. Be careful not to let emotions lead the conversation either. They can cloud your common sense and cause you to ignore Holy Spirit who has been talking to you anyway which is why you are at this point. Push them (your emotions) aside and think logically. Your destiny is on the line here so take this seriously. It's time for you to break free.

Step 2: Listen to that little voice (holy spirit) that is telling you move on!

Do not ignore the nudging deep within that is telling you to move your life forward. Own up to your mistakes, emotions and longings for this person. Being honest with yourself and what you want will help you make a clear decision as to why you need to move on. In all reality, you've been telling yourself " this just doesn't feel right" anyway.

Step 3: Make a choice!

Decide what you really want and compare it to what you have. See the difference? Having mixed emotions is apart of the process in the makeup to breakup relationship. You have to let those emotions die. They are mixed up and mismanaged which is why you keep going back. You can't keep feeding them the same poison and expect to become well. Now this isn't easy, but it's worth it, and you deserve it. Don't forget that!

Step 4: Realize that fear is #1 a liar, and you're going to overcome it.

You real fear is that you're going to be alone, and that you "need" someone to be in your life. LIES! Be ok with enjoying just YOU. Give each other space and face the fear head on. This will give you both time to think clearly without the cloudiness of each other's company which will only sparks those emotions back up that we are no longer going to entertain. Remember we are working towards ending the cycle.

Step 5: Stand firm on your decision.
You have made up your mind now and you don't need to go backwards ANYMORE. Pray

for strength and wisdom and most importantly let God show you how much he loves you and what he wants for you. You don't have to look back once you have committed to moving forward. That little voice hasn't lied to you. Its waiting on you to make your move so you can have WHO you deserve.

What you won't let go of is holding you back, not being able to identify the root is holding you back. Be 100% sure that some cycles can be created by you and others you inherit through your blood line, but NOTHING is too bad for the power of God. I MEAN NOTHING!

Chapter 11. True Love is God's Love on Replay

"Husbands, love your wives, just as Christ loved the church and gave himself up for her"

Ephesians 5:25

On my journey to becoming better I've learned something's mainly with guys, but I've learned none the less.

I want you to imagine a man who loved you so much he gave up his life for you. This scripture always reminds me how I should be loved. I've watched my surroundings try influence me to believe marriage is about what is in his pocket and not his heart. It is his heart for God that will always make a man more attractive than his bank account. It is his example of surrender to God that should show me his intentions. A man's money can't buy salvation or cover a woman in prayer. Success without Jesus is not impressive to a woman who knows she's worth more rubies and especially to woman who knows how to make her own coins!

Guys are consumed with money and careers. There are guys that get caught up in the idea that they need money to be a "man." God ordained men to labor, which means He was going to supply what was needed to financially take care of a family. I understand the burden that men feel to be financially stable based on the mandate placed on men. If God gave men such a mandate, shouldn't they seek Him for the income? At least that's what I would like to think

When I bartended in the clubs or went for a night of fun, I'll be honest, we all looked for the booth with the ballers. I've seen girls stand at the bar while I was working and try to get the attention of the guy spending the most money. The guys would buy the most bottles of alcohol, typically the most expensive bottle of champagne. Music pushed these men to believe they can be " ballers" like common rappers.

Growth showed me I needed to be more like Lydia in the Bible. She had her own business, she was hospitable and a prayer warrior. As I grew to know God, she became my inspiration. Then there is Esther the Queen of Queens. She went from overlooked, abandoned, and unqualified, to the Queen who delivers the oppressed, broken, and lost.

God gave us role models way before the examples media tried to push on us. As you identify who you are in Christ, you know your purpose and direction. A woman needs someone who can cover her in prayer, daily. She needs prayer with you and confidence that you are covering her when you're apart. She needs protection and direction. The men were called to be the head for a reason.

One major issue with my past relationships was that they weren't practicing believers. I was submitted, and they didn't even so much as attend church or read their Bible. There was such a clash in beliefs and morals.

When I say practicing, I mean they have submitted themselves to leadership and created a covering for themselves; they pray, worship, serve, and diligently seek God through His word. There aren't too many guys I've dated that take this thing I have with Jesus as serious as I do. Now they don't have to be on "level," and I am not saying I am better than them. They just get caught up in beauty and the great exploits they see, but they ARE NOT equipped to handle all of the woman God has made her to be. They are clueless about who they are themselves.

The best gift someone can give you is lifting your name to the Father above in Prayer. If we cannot go before God together in prayer how can we go any further. We must seek God separately, but also together if we plan on finding out His will. Prayer reveals the answers we often forget to seek. I remember when I prayed and asked God to show my mentee if she should be with the guy she was with. God sent her a dream where her spiritual mother said to her he's not the one. She was able to walk away 100% sure.

If you feel there's something missing, here is what you do before you just cut them off: Pray and ask God to reveal to you your purpose in life and the purpose of your partner. You may be with your soul mate but at the wrong time. Taking time to grow separately is a GREAT thing. Know the difference between your soulmate and someone with a different purpose.

Discern what season of life you are in. Look closely at your life and identify what is most important. Is it your career, family, love, or relationship? Seek guidance from people that you trust in your life, like a mentor. And ultimately, ask God to show you what He wants to produce *through* you in His season.

Make sure you are in fact the person God wants you to be. God didn't call you to just work, raise kids, and die. He has a purpose for you even if you don't think so. He wants you to include Him in all the details relationships included. BE BRAVE ENOUGH to walk away. Your destiny is on the line ladies and gentlemen. If your holding on to someone God doesn't want you to have. Its ok to just be friends or nothing at all. They just may not be called to your life. Fellas if you happen to take the time to read this and you really want to know the secret to a woman's heart, it's locked up in the heart of God. Be like David, a man after God's own heart, or like Jacob devoted to obtaining ONE woman, and God will connect you to the heart that is for you. What a woman needs from her man is for him to complete her destiny. This CANNOT be bought with cash, it's bought with your surrender to Christ.

What we all really want is someone WHOLE with a clear VISION. We all need and desire balance and God's grace, love, and direction will get us there.

Chapter 12. Private Pain, Don't Suffer in Silence

I don't always have good days. Some days I am dealing with some real, private pain. This is heavy on my heart, and I want to encourage not only myself, but also you. Be mindful that under the top layers of what you see, is a story you may never get to read.

What is private pain? It's the things you don't talk about, the weight you carry that no one knows about. It's the tears you cry behind closed doors after the long day of work, class, business, being a spouse, a friend, or a parent. It's the pain from the friend who stabbed you in the back or the relationship that ended, the money that ran dry, the insecurity, the unanswered questions, the guilt, shame, fear, daddy who left you, mommy who doesn't love you, family that's broken, ministry that's suffering, business that isn't growing, the empty promises, self-doubt, suicidal thoughts, depression.

That's the pain I am speaking about. You don't mention it to anyone or talk about. It's the pain that causes you to come home and throw yourself before God, and cry out to Him, "Why God?"

If we can all be real we all sometimes question him. We know we have to have faith to please him (Hebrew 11:6) and not focus on what we see (Hebrew 11:1). We can be believing for our bills to be paid, but our accounts are in the negative. That is when Faith kicks in. We don't know how but we trust and believe God will supply.

We know the plans He has for us are for good and not for disaster. We know He gives us a future and hope (Jeremiah 29:11).
We know all of this but even in the midst of knowing this we still have this pain. Why?

One major pain I dealt with heavily was that no man would marry me. After my broken engagement, I began to believe every guy would just leave me. My issue with rejection was real and I needed it to be broken. Don't be afraid to go through a deliverance process. The process will get to the root of your issues, identify all demons and strongholds, and set you free. You can be released from the pillows full of tears, in pain from rejection—not just from men but even friends. I was often dropped for doing nothing but loving hard. When you are constantly misunderstood, misread, and assumed to be something you are not, it takes a toll on your heart. I remember telling God if it's just me and You forever that's fine, just take this pain from me. I remember dealing with the guilt and pain of my life all by myself in my bedroom, just believing it would one day change. We all have been there.

It's in this pain you will find your strength. It's when you hit rock bottom, tears flowing, broken before God, crying out, is where he does his best work. This is a very vulnerable place, yet a rewarding place to be. Rewarding because this is where transformation occurs.

It's ok to be broken to be built back up. God sees you trying your best. He sees you getting back up each and every time you get the wind knocked out of you. It's in your press that you're going to be blessed! He wants you to trust him through this process even when it hurts. He is refining, and making you new.

WE ALL WIN! We all in win God. Scripture says we can do all things this include overcoming pain (Philippians 4:13).

I can do all things through him who strengthens me. This includes pain. Pain doesn't. Pain is temporary, it won't last forever. That thing you are dealing with in private is going to make you shine in HIS glory publicly. People will see you shining not knowing it was God. Then you can the testimony. You're an OVERCOMER, just walk it out.

> *"I have told you these things, so that in me you may have peace. In this world, you will have trouble. But take heart! I have overcome the world."*
>
> John 16:33

The pain of the past doesn't go away. It has to be dealt with, so while I have attempted to move forward, I may have not properly healed. Pray, fast, break ties, and be free. Love needs time to grow.

Chapter 13. Fall Back

You fall back not off. It is ok to pull your heart out of a situation and think clearer. When you can take your emotions out of dating it will allow you to make sound decisions. This allows you to think and make more sound decisions. We are often told to follow our hearts. However,

The heart is deceitful above all things, and desperately sick; who can understand it?

Jeremiah 17:9 states ESV

After a whole year since my broken engagement, getting back into the "dating" field is pretty tricky yet rewarding. If your smart you take this time to learn exactly what you don't want and how not to let history repeat itself.

Did I start dating again after the split? Yes, I sure did and it was not to find love just to stay busy. For me dating was helpful and kept my focus off my ex, but didn't lead me to prince charming AT ALL. It did however lead me into another phase of self-discovery with God. Every time I dated someone I learned something new about how God loved me so much He would protect my destiny from the wrong man.

So, at this time, I was introduced to the online dating world. If you have ever tried it, you know it can a headache and blessing. My mother actually met her husband through online dating as did my cousin so I stand by it 100% however be very careful. I will share those tips with you all a little later.

I get on a site. I meet one guy who was very handsome. We go out to dinner and hit it off instantly! So, I'm like, really? Real people and fine men use this to date? We just might have something here. We went to dinner, and then headed downtown to a hookah bar for more drinks and conversation. We seemed to have so much in common, and both were looking for someone to hang out with.

Now here's where things get tricky. He was a great guy, awesome manners, knew how to treat a lady, and everything. The rubber met the road though, and I had to let him go. He was not of the same faith as me. He was a Jehovah's Witness.

One thing I will NOT compromise is JESUS. He must be in your heart, and you must know Him if you plan on dating me. We can be friends and have different faiths but not romantic partners.

One thing I began to focus on was learning to hear God's voice clearly. On a particular night, and I remember it like yesterday, God said to me, "I'm protecting you from him." Now I was like, "Huh?" I literally heard those words in my inner ear, "I'm protecting you from him."

Then I prayed and prayed. My prayer was, "God not my will but Yours!" I knew It was time to cut the cord of connection and walk away.

God began to reveal things to me about this guy I really didn't want to know. He had a record from domestic abuse, he was liar, and I found out later he had a baby on the way. The young lady found me online, messaged me, and we even chatted on the phone. I even took the time to minister her. I let her know, "woman to woman," how much value she held and how she too could find a man who would love her and not lie to her. I let her know a few more things prophetically and then released her from line.

I knew I was surely leaving him. There was no question about that. One thing I don't play with is Godly warning. Satan and his minions tried to snatch me at this VERY vulnerable place in my life. He thought if he could give me what I wanted, minus Jesus, I would just leave God and go with this man. I desired to be loved, but I ultimately desired the love of Jesus.

God doesn't want us to be led blindly so simply asking Him to show you or tell you will make this process easy. I would meet guys who were really nice guys, but they weren't MY GUY. I even met a virgin, awesome man of God, but honey not my man of God. I'm not perfect by any means, but even the best of guys has some stuff with them. What "stuff" are you willing to look past is the question and what "stuff" have you been called to partner with.

BE CLEAR ON WHAT YOU WANT AND DON'T COMPROMISE.

I'm not saying when you meet someone, he will be packaged completely the way you want him to be. But you will know when you are wasting time.

Emotions of excitement cloud your vision and discernment. Things could be going great but it always ok to pull your heart out

of a situation to get your mind right.
Remember this is lifetime commitment.
2 Corinthians 10:5 ESV

On my journey of becoming who God wanted
me to be "Holy" separate, and sacred. I had to also
deal with Satan sending me men who would try to
influence me out of my Christian faith. There was once
a Muslim man as well. He equally was just as an
amazing guy as this one. While you are on the journey
temptations come. When you are vulnerable Satan tries
his best to trip you up. As Jesus Fasted, Satan came to
test him too. Jesus was vulnerable because he was
Fasting. You never know when your season of testing
is coming. Be sure to fill yourself with the word of
God so it will come into remembrance and you won't
sin against God.
Jesus countered with another citation from
Deuteronomy:

"Don't you dare test the Lord your God."
Matthew 4:7 The Message (MSG)

Even when the test gets heavy, and you are
tempted to stray away, TRUST that God has angels on
assignment to rescue you and take care of your needs.

Chapter 14. Worth More Than What They See

I can remember being a young girl, and my mother always would say to my sisters and myself "know your worth ladies, what you have within you is worth more than diamonds." When you look at the value of a diamond or a diamond ring you think of a jewelry store. The diamond is protected by a glass. The glass has a lock on it. Only those with the key could access the diamond.

Abstinence for me has been a way for me to reconnect with my true self, and God. Its helped me see clearly how pre-marital sex was trying to ruin parts of my life. Dating men had been my safe haven. It was a way for me to feel safe due to the absence of my father from my life. He wasn't absent the entire time. Through choosing to abstain from sex and actually read my Bible my life began to change for the better and that's what ill be addressing throughout this book. From friendships, career, school and most importantly dating, God has used dating as a vital key to my transformation and self-discovery.

So, here's the tricky part. Even after I decided to abstain from sex I slipped up and fell back in bed with a guy a loved. The conviction was so heavy, God interrupted us right in the middle. Yes, in the middle of intercourse. I broke down in tears and simply told him, "I can't do this." He understood, unlike most guys. Abstinence wasn't his thing, but he respected me, loved me, and still does until this day (as a friend).

Give abstinence a try and see how clear things will become in your life. I've done it, went backwards and got back on track. Stay focused its truly worth it and the best birth control out!

Don't be the one who dates the married, engaged, or committed because he makes you feel good, says the right things, or makes empty promises, yes empty! IT IS A TRAP. You're not only disrespecting yourself, but his innocent partner, and most importantly God. God is a God of covenant. You, man and HIM. When you disrupt covenant, you disrespect the holy union God had brought together. You pervert his plan

Everything he does to and for you, he is doing for his wife if not more. Think about it, your stomach flipped, didn't it?

You shouldn't think that sneaking to be with someone is acceptable. Dating someone that is with another woman is unethical.

It's not, and it's out of order. Perhaps if we had more single women who stood up these men and sent them back to their wives we just may bring the amount of cheating down.

You can't be an Esther and live like Olivia, always finding yourself in a scandal. You deserve to be #1, not #2.

A real man can recognize your weaknesses and will makes it his business to build you up in those areas. He will see your insecurities and provide security, he will see your baggage and help you unpack, he will recognize he is to protect and cover you.

A REAL man of God respects your purity. I promise you ladies if you hold off you will be able to get rid of a lot of counterfeits that are only out for your goodies. Sexual intercourse brings so many emotions, that before marriage the relationship isn't ready to handle. You end up feeling connected to someone God never intended you to be with in the first place.

Ever find it hard to walk away from a relationship you knew was wrong? It's called a soul tie: a spiritual/emotional connection you have to someone after being intimate with them, usually engaging in sexual intercourse.

Even when you are far away from them, and out of their presence. You still feel as if they are a part of you, and apart of you is with them. This then causes you to feel incomplete. Almost as if you've given up some of yourself that cannot be easily possessed again. When it's a pure connection from God you have peace, the connection doesn't distract you from God. You don't feel like you have lost anything, you actually gain.

You don't have a price tag of $100 dinners, $300 shoes, $1500 purse, or even worse, a $1 being throw at you while you show the world your most sacred gifts. You are priceless! The price a man pays for you is marriage. Honor yourself and hold yourself in high standard, because you ARE that valuable. A man will treat you based off how you value YOURSELF.

If you show it all, you leave nothing for him to imagine. Then you wonder why he treats you like the gum on the bottom of his shoe. Many time women will see a guy they have dated treat the next woman better than he treated her. Did you ever stop to think he valued her because she FIRST valued herself?

It starts with you. You have to make a decision. You either want the BEST or you don't. You either want to be #1 or just a number. You either wanted to be treated like a Queen or a peasant. The choice is yours. Stop believing the lies that you aren't good enough, pretty enough, skinny enough, because God says you are ENOUGH. God is head over heels in love with you and I, and desires for us to be loved the way he loves us. If We can stand firm on this truth, knowing that God will send us a mate that will honor us we can really change things in the "dating world". Don't get caught up on what others are doing and delight in the promise that it is our inner beauty that pleases God and the man he has for you will see that same beauty.

Instead, it should be that of your inner self, the unfading beauty of a gentle and quiet spirit, which is of great worth in Gods sight.

1 Peter 3:4

Chapter 15. You Lost Me When You Lied

I think we have all experienced a liar or two or TEN! The thing about someone lying to you that hurts the most, is that they don't believe you deserve the truth. I love God, and we have a tight relationship. God really is the most loyal person on my team, and He never hides things from me. God hold no secrets from me.

I came across a young woman, beautiful girl who just happened to spend a little too much time on the page of a guy I was dating. Since I'm far from the jealous type, I sat on this check in my spirit for about two months.

Then one day I said, "You know what, it's time to find out what I already know." The beauty of having a relationship with God is He speaks to you. She and I began to converse and in the midst of a conversation via Instagram.

I found out they were "kicking it." She said they weren't dating, and she didn't want him, but she made it clear that it was "something," so much so that he had just been by her home a week and half prior. She told me everything.

She didn't value herself, unfortunately. I knew she would continue her relationship with him. They normally do. But here is why I tried to believe her anyways: she didn't know I already knew months' prior that something was going on. He started doing

79

little things like not calling at night as normal. He would delete post that I commented on and then make up a bogus story as to why.

She had a text message to prove him denying his relationship with me, and I had one saying the same against her. She wasn't mad. She was pleasant, respectful, and was more concerned about her children being lied to than herself. He had met her daughters, and she mention to me that the youngest one would ask often where he was.

She wasn't a broke down desperate woman, she was woman who was deceived as well. She was a woman who was once me, but she actually was married when her husband denied his relationship with her and went his way. She had no reason to want to be the other woman after her ex mingled with the women who destroyed her marriage.

I was PISSED! He lied and continued to lie. A lie is something that could make me lose ALL respect for you. He made up elaborate stories of her being jealous, and some woman from his past. I knew better though. I let him try to redeem himself, but he would rather lie and continue lying. After my grace period ran out for him, I had a choice to make. I made the choice to leave no ties no nothing. I can't trust a liar.

He was to was pastor who was highly anointed by God to do kingdom work. Gifts come without repentance. The anointing breaks the yolk, the anointing is the only qualification for marriage. We would talk all night, fall asleep on Facetime, go to services together. I was blinded by my feelings—

I'll be honest. I just knew, he was it. I was blind to the narcissistic traits he had.

Narcissism, involves cockiness, manipulatives, selfishness, power motives, and vanity—a love of mirrors. How do you know if you're in fact in a relationship with a narcissist? Here are few key things to look for.

1. Acting like they are the trophy of the relationship
2. Sweet talking to get what they want
3. Everyone else comes last
4. Making decisions for you that's good for them.

So, after I let the dust settled, I was able to see clearly. He was too busy trying to "cover" himself. He didn't care how he that caused hurt, the lies he told. He just wanted me to believe the nonsense and attempt to make it work. I am just not built like that. So, if you are having a hard time walking away from the table when the truth is no longer on the menu, follow these tips:

Seek wise counsel. Not your single home girls either.
I talked to people with wisdom and much to my surprised they advised me to pray, and if the truth was given we may could work it out. Against my normal judgement, I agreed. The thing is what we had was bigger than a mistake or so I thought. I had it in my heart to forgive him and move on effectively. I cannot however

build a house on a weak foundation of lies and deceit.

Pray and ask God to make the purpose clear.
Why is this happening? Did I miss something? What would you have to come from this God? Your answers are in prayer and worship.

Any love less than His is not more portion. God calls men to love their wives as Christ loved the church, and well I wasn't feeling like the church at all.

Don't Budge
Once you have decided what you
can and cannot live with, don't budge. Don't be persuaded into the game or "charming chatter." If he will do everything yet not tell you the truth, stay firm and keep it moving.

Allow yourself to heal.
It may hurt, but don't let your emotions drive you back into the arms of who lied to you.

Chapter 16. The Last and Final Counterfeit

T here came a time where I decided to be INTENTIONALLY single. I knew I had a lot to produce purpose wise and my husband was coming therefore I didn't want nor need a distraction in the form of a man.

Then I received a message from a pretty influential Online Pastor asking me to email him my number. He messaged me on Instagram, but this was only for a date clarification on him coming to NC to preach. He then asked for my email. At this time, I assumed to be put on an email blast regarding engagements.

> Him: *Hi just received your email on Instagram, how are you?"*
>
> Me: *Hi Pastor, I am well thank you for asking. How are you?*
>
> Him: *I'm well so what are you up to in life? You have an awesome page....*

We went back and for several emails about what I do, his upcoming travel, laughs about me being an over packer and then I reeled the conversation back to the dates he had scheduled to preach. I didn't want to get off track. The real reason we were chatting was to solidify dates for his preaching engagement.

Him: *lol that's funny I bet you could pack the world! I have two dates one in charlotte and one in Sandford ...The dates are TBA*

Me: *"I'll try to make at least one."*

So, at this point I'm confused as to why he needed to email me dates he didn't have. But I charged it to the, "He's a nice Pastor just connecting with the people" card.

That's the end of that conversation. The next few months go by, and I began to notice him coming onto my IG page, randomly liking my photos. Which was weird, because he didn't follow me. He actually doesn't follow anyone on his IG page.

Later I received a message from him on Facebook. This time after conversing about one of his empowerment calls he shifted into asking me to email him some time again soon and that he'll send his number.

Now at this point I'm well aware he didn't want to exchange numbers to text-pals. HE WAS OFFICIALLY interested. I was too. We chatted from that day forward literally EVERYDAY. From text, to calls, and Facetime was his favorite, especially early in the morning. He was fascinated by how pretty I was first thing in the morning with no makeup. Our conversations ended often with "stay beautiful." Every conversation was dope, funny, insightful, and refreshing.

I would be lying if I said I wasn't digging him because I WAS! So much I mentioned him to my

Mentor, Mom and Pastor. They are my safety net. Notice how I didn't say my homegirls. Now they knew, but I know who to get wisdom from regarding certain situations.

My birthday came on 4/17. He called me and sang happy birthday. Then we chatted for a while, and he said things that confirmed prophetic words I had gotten literally hours before regarding my one day husband. Now, I'm looking at my phone like, *Huh, what?* He doesn't even know what he said nor the significance... or does he?

He has a fascination with planes jets in particular, oddly enough I do too. I spend some of my work days silently in the cut watching them take off. There were so many things we had in common. He loves water, so do I. One of the words I received was that my husband would show me how to be a spokesperson. He told me to do an infomercial for practice as if I was on the radio. Not because I told him the word either, it just came out his mouth one day.

Then I had the chance to meet him in person. Yes, all this time all we had was facetime. My sister needed my family in NJ one weekend, and he lives in NY so it was perfect. I told my mom, and she jokingly kept saying we were going on a date.

I was like, "Nah, nah we are just meeting up, nothing serious."

Later that evening as I arrived to my hotel he sends me this:

"Hey thanks for being beautiful, prophetic, and powerful addition to my life. I'm trusting you and thanking God for you. Know that I enjoyed every moment, and I'm thankful for your vision".

After a wonderful night, he proceeded to make me an admin on his VERY busy Facebook page. There are at least 1.2 million people following him or more. I was honored to help and took this as sign of him showing me he trusted me...and well I could trust him too. There was nothing to hide, right?

I would help him manage the page and his live messages. This is when things changed. You know someone's true colors eventually come through.

I've seen more than I would have liked. His "email" tactic was uncovered VERY quickly. Now I am a woman of wisdom, so I don't just jump on the handle and accuse anyone of anything. Life carried on as usual, but I made a mental note of everything.

April was gone, we met in May, and then he came to NC in June at the end of his ninety-day probation. Now I am impressed he made it this far. Again, I was intentionally single and could sniff a fake from miles away.

But June was different. We met in his hometown in Fayetteville where he grew up. We spent the day together. We ate at an Italian spot downtown, walked around, he recorded a live video, and we visited his brothers. One in particular had a baby on the way. Sweet couple. I remember him playing some song on the piano that was hilarious and then the guys went swimming while the ladies watched.

During the evening, we were sitting on the couch at his mom's house. I saw a message come through his phone saying, "I just love you so much." I made a HUGE mental note. I then asked him to be honest and tell if he was seeing anyone else. He said no. He was adamant about the fact that he wasn't. I let it go for the night but didn't let what I saw go. We kept talking through the night and fell asleep on the couch. The next day we parted ways and went back to our norm. No sex, just two tired people.

I then saw on social media where he had become friends with the name I saw in his phone that evening. He proceeded to act as if he didn't know that I knew what was up. I was able to use social media to connect the dots. Then I took some time to myself. I let him know I needed no contact for at least a week.

I fasted and prayed! Then I finally asked him, "Why did you lie? Now our friendship was nothing but a blur."

He responded saying it wasn't and asked me if I wanted to talk. July 19th was our last conversation. He made up some hogwash about always being rejected by women. Remember, this is the same guy with 1,828,348,328,191 women in his inbox. He then began to share what he thought was the truth. He made it clear that "it wasn't that deep" with whomever he was talking. He then began to express his heart and tell me everything, days, moments, and hours WAY TOO LATE. I wasn't having it though. His truth was the half-truth, but I was glad God showed me the parts he left out. Unfortunately, I had to forgive him and move on.

I remember a comment he made that makes sense now " I would have to marry a woman who owns her own business or teaches." His now girlfriend was a teacher. I guess he was weighing his options without letting us know.

I messaged his girlfriend with NO INTENT for them to breakup but every woman deserves the truth. Granted she didn't hear the 40-minute conversation I had with him. If she desired more truth I would've happily given it to her. What she did after was her choice.

He tried to make it seem as if he wasn't pursuing anyone. I let him know that day I could not even be his friend anymore. I had to do this for me. He felt I was being selfish. When it comes to protecting my heart, I have to be selfish. He couldn't hear what I heard. He wanted me to forget everything and just be his friend while he shifted in his pursuit without letting me know. He messed up when he moved on without first telling me. The conversation became really intense. I had tears in my eyes and asked him to please just leave me alone and to relinquish my friendship. Spiritually he expressed his "need" for me. I apparently "helped him more than I knew."

He said, "This will heal. I love you, and I thank God for you Jennifer even though you don't see it."

And that was the last day we conversed.

I learned a lot from this ordeal and to be 100% honest, it shook my faith. At that time and in my mind, I was not good enough for him. My rejection flared privately. I spent a lot of time talking to God. I was prophetically discouraged and confused. No one would ever know it unless you were close to me. The woman who encouraged everyone was DEEPLY discouraged, depressed, and fighting a war that could only be won in prayer.

Deliverance is vital don't be ashamed of it, if you don't receive it you should be ashamed of that. There's no greater feeling then purging it out of your spirit. That's what I did. I prayed and purged myself through tears and deep breaths. Not just from his rejection, but from ALL OF IT, from anyone or a previous event.

When you share your testimony, two people become FREE. You and someone else. I couldn't be selfish, I just had to be vulnerable enough to let you know I too get hurt and go through trials and what was my way of escape.

I prayed for her, for her heart, mind, spirit, happiness and that she wouldn't feel what I felt. It's never ok to be mad at the other woman. I actually felt bad. My heart went out to her in hope that she NEVER experienced what I had. I lifted her and asked God to protect her heart.

All this time and it began to hit me: I was aiming way too low. God has so much better for me. Sometimes God says no because we aim too low. It's insulting to his Power. I love the song, "When Jesus Says Yes, Nobody can Say No," by Michelle Williams.

"Without consultation, plans are frustrated, But with many counselors they succeed."
Proverbs 15:22

We are planning to be great spouses, but not inviting the right people to assist us in being successful with the plan. We can get caught up on what we see on the outside, the great attempts they make trying

to impress you, and forget to ask God
for His permission and insight. God started showing
me things, and I was like, "Oh no, Sir."

Now we all have our stuff, but we are made
specifically for someone's stuff too. So, I prayed, and
God even used people to tell me
"Baby girl, no. Don't waste your time."

Even in church there are guys who
just aren't for you. I don't want anyone to think just
because you stop meeting them at bars and clubs that
all of sudden they become angels. Men are MEN! You
have to be careful no matter where they FIND YOU!

God's "No" is not rejection, but
redirection. God's "no" to one thing is a "yes" to
another. In 2 Sam 7, God said "no" to David's desire to
build a temple.

I always thought to make it my education would
frame my life. But what is education without purpose?
When I asked God to help fulfill a degree thinking
paper, He said no. God used different avenues to let
me know my life would be just a little different.

*Those things don't define you. I define you.
Here is the roadmap of entrepreneurship.*

God told me no to school but still gave me a yes
to building my own business. God's "no" isn't
punishment, it's preparation. Rom 5:2a-5 states, "And
we rejoice in the hope of the glory of God. Not only
so, but we also rejoice in our sufferings, because we
know that suffering produces perseverance;

perseverance, character; and character, hope. And hope does not disappoint us, because God has poured out His love into our hearts by the Holy Spirit, whom He has given us."

God is preparing us to be His Son's bride. We will reign with Him; we must be bride worthy of our position. He develops perseverance, character, and hope as we trust Him in prayer. Prayer and spiritual warfare is His means of preparing us for bridehood.

Good Girl, Gone Bad, Gone Holy

Chapter 17. Prepare for a Love Worth Waiting

N ow that I've seen all the counterfeits, learned all the lessons and most importantly become even closer to God. It is preparation time for the real thing.

As women, we think we have it all together. Career, car, home, good credit. But there may be something you've missed! Make sure you are ready to mature for who God has in mind for you. How are you going to give your life to someone, and you don't know what you are giving in return? Are you positioned for the pursuit?

Now when I say positioned, I don't only mean in the physical sense. Anyone, and I do mean anyone, can look the part. But what does your heart look like? Are you completely over the last guy who hurt you? Have you healed from daddy wounds? Are you open to new love? Or do you still have a brick wall guarding your heart because you feel like you need to be protected?

You can't be unnecessarily difficult and expect them to just understand or put up with it. NEWS FLASH most wont. GET HEALED. Be vulnerable enough to seek deliverance, and be free from ALL demonic strongholds that would stop you from the love you desire.

Have you considered the fact that God can be protecting his sons from a woman like you? God doesn't want to bless his young Kings with Queens who haven't even realized that they are just that, a

Queen. I think we all can get too consumed with a man coming and fixing us that we don't fix ourselves.

An idle mind is a devil's playground. Ladies, don't sit around thinking a man is going to show up and just change your life when you don't have one. Get focused on your purpose. You were put here on this earth to do things. You can change the world with your natural/spiritual gifts and talents.

YOU DON'T NEED TO BE RESCUED by a man. Let your purpose RESCUE you! Your purpose will fulfill you! How do you know what your purpose is?

What did you desire as a child to be as you grew older? All of these things play a major role in your purpose. It's not just what makes you money, but also what makes you HAPPY!

So, bottom line: GET BUSY! A woman who is busy about her God ordained purpose is fulfilled and confident in what is to come. There are things you are NOT willing to compromise or at least shouldn't. SO, DON'T! We all have our thing, whether it's no sex, a man that has no relationship with God, and the list could go on. As long as your deal breakers are reasonable and not petty, don't budge. Men like strong women who know what they want. Who wants a push over? REAL men need strong women of great wisdom. They are going to consider you as someone who will possibly raise their daughter or son one day. We are reflections of our Father God. He's told us who we are.

Become a Proverbs 31 woman: You are hard to find. you aren't easily accessible by just anyone, for your worth exceeds rubies. Some of our issue, ladies, is that we are accessible to options of men who would never suit us. So why are we wasting time! You don't need company or comfort from just anyone.

Let me paint the picture for you. You are in ministry and at the club hoping to find your husband. Now he could be there, but if you are called to be a pastor's wife, do you really think he would be there? Gems are found in odd places, sometimes they even miraculously appear. Let God let you miraculously appear to the man He has for you. Don't be for sale.

Ladies be clear and take pride in the fact that you are his crown, he honors you. To honor you, you must be trustworthy. Can he trust you? Can you be trusted with money? Caring for the home? More importantly his flaws—can he trust you not to throw his shortcomings back at him during the most frivolous dispute? Can you be his safe place in the midst of chaos? Can he come to you and find strength? Ask yourself these questions and take a deep look inside.

Get up start your day, pray, be organized, and have purpose to your day. You will one day do this for your family. Master it alone first! I am currently not married and my list is the boss of my day. Practice now because your purposed driven, multifaceted life will be paired one day to a man and children He will be depending on you to be his superwoman. Grab the cape now!

Yea your single you don't live with your husband. You should be practicing now how to keep your home in order so your mind is in order. Can you cook? Clean? Are you consistent with small stuff like making your bed? No? Then start practicing now. Do you really want to share your space with anyone?

Imagine that on a daily. I don't know about you, but I love my space and I'll enjoy it alone as long as God sees fit. With a husband, and then kids.

Life is NEVER just about you. You can help someone in the smallest ways. The people on the side of the roads need someone too. It's as simple as taking your leftovers and packing them up to intentionally bless someone at some point in the day. Let's be real: Most of us cook way more food than we can eat and it gets wasted. Help someone bless them with your EXTRA. Serve at a shelter, have a blanket drive, donate clothes, read to the elderly whatever you do just makes sure you help someone else.

Men are visual. You don't have or show your boobies but show class, STYLE, and grace. If you don't know what to do with your hair, style of dress, ask someone. It's ok not to know what you need to do. Help yourself, and ladies if you have it together help your sisters out. I am an image consultant I'll gladly help you find your inner diva.

Lastly of all the woman in the world she who is most worthy of praise is the woman who fears God. Get right with God ladies you're so precious. Seek him first. You don't want to settle just because Johnny liked your Facebook photo and invited you to dinner. Take time to qualify him before you go any further.

Chapter 18. My Better Dream

I see my future coming and this is your welcome letter. Welcoming you into the next phase of our destiny and showing me what I once forget on exist. This is like the welcome letter you get before you go to college letting you know you are accepted.

I'm accepting you. Accepting every part of you. When I read your application, your past experiences, you were qualified for a lifetime of no judgment, your fears qualified you for a love that would heal the wounds that caused it, and your accomplishments made me blush at what an honor it's going to be, to be your side.

Now there was only one application available for this position so trust me, I didn't choose between you and the second best. I left the spot open and prayed for God to navigate your pen to my paper because I needed a God chaser in my life. There's something in you that's going to pull ME out.

I gave up on you, I thought you didn't exist, I settled in my heart many days with tears coming down my face. Myself and God was all I had in the end.

There really wasn't a reason to cry because God was sending me a very best friend.

I've heard so much about you already. Your prominence will announce your arrival, your mantle with be able to manage the masses and will make me sure. I've patiently waited, watched, and warred for you. I've planted the seed of prayer you place in my life in good ground, and I am letting it come into fruition. I'm currently hidden. I asked God to give you the roadmap to find me. I gave him specific details so

you don't get lost. I prayed protection from the
Jezebels and Delilahs, because I know now how
important it is for us to unite.

It will be an honor to meet you. It's my duty to
be your safe place. To serve you will be my delight,
and to love you is my pleasure. I'm going through altar
alterations before my dress alteration is to be ready for
a lifetime and not a just a moment.

Finding my way to myself all started with the
idea and practice of abstinence. It started with me
preparing myself to be a bride. Instead God decided to
perfect me to his bride first. With my plan and Gods, I
collided into my destiny. I'm ready for the next levels
of success, the next level of true friendship, the growth
in my family. The next level is of spiritual
enlightenment and the introduction to Gods love
manifest in a man.

I hope now that you have read some of my
journey, and that you understand that the
journey isn't about being perfect. It is about learning
along the way.

God is so faithful He will even use the crooked
path we take to land us back on His track. Since men
were the one thing the enemy used to grab my
attention, God did too. The overall search was
for acceptance. Rejection makes you simply look for
people who accept you through bad friendships I was
able to learn that your community will determine your
commute. It makes more sense than ever that who you
surround yourself with has a positive influence on your
life. He allowed me to find another level of my worth
and grow spiritually. I am more than clear now, that I
am called to encourage women in self-worth and

identity. Nothing I've went through or learned is in vain. God took my pursuit and led me back to Him. God will really finish what He has started in you.

Chapter 19: With Purpose, Become

I had to learn the beauty and contentment in being with Jesus. Being single isn't a death sentence. It's an opportunity to truly connect with God. If you are single and reading this enjoy the journey. If you are married and reading this stay connected to God. Don't let anything come in between that relationship.

No matter how bad it gets there is always a part two. Hold on, this chapter will end soon.

Know their worth and NEVER settle.

Look at adversity with a smile and press forward. When they hated, I smiled, when was I told *no* I smiled, when I was denied jobs I smiled, when I spent a weekend in jail, I smiled and prayed for the women inside, when guys didn't know my worth, I smiled. While I waited to be set free, I SMILED.

Adversity reminds me that there is always a brighter side and some of the very things we complain about, someone wished that was their only complaint.

For Women who have experienced criminal records, lack of funding for school, domestic violence, the wrong friends, one parent homes, or anything that is what society says is "set back," let me be the first to remind you: It's truly setting you up. Put your trust fully in God and watch him turn it around. Take that first step of changing the defeat and doubt in your mind and turn it into DETERMINATION AND DRIVE.

Here are some tips and strategies I will leave you with as you derive your purpose and in turn, secure your future destiny:

1. Discern quickly!
Listen to how they are speaking and take notes. The enemy is tricky, so things may seem to be "lining up." But you need to keep track so you can see where things don't!

2. Pray, pray, pray, and did I say pray?
Prayer is COMMUNICATION with God. He can answer you quickly too.

3. Tell people who you trust to pray.
They can intercede to see what God shows them. Hold yourself accountable and keep yourself covered.

4. FAST!
It's amazing what a quick fast can show you. Give me three days, I'll know what I need to know.

5. Accept the NO.
Thank God for it. Stay praying until the right one comes along.

Now I won't say what I went through made me give up on online dating. I dabbled in it a little more, but one thing you will find is there are a lot of short guys on there. No disrespect but I'm not a short guy kind of girl. There are also a lot of creeps so the block button becomes your best friend. Lastly there are a lot of guys that aren't following God themselves so they could never lead me. So, if you decide to go this route here are a few things to keep in mind and look out for.

1. Look at the photos!
Some guys use fake photos, and you can tell. Especially the guys with just one photo. RED FLAG!

2. Do not give out your phone number quickly!
The message system is just as good as texting. Take your time, and if need be get a Google Plus number so you don't have to worry about them having your real number.

3. DO NOT (and this a big one) meet anyone without screening them!
Use Facebook, Instagram, Skype, and Glide. Confirm who this person is. See what connections you have via social media/friends etc. I would always Facetime or use sometime of visual video aid to confirm they were the guy before meeting.

4. NEVER meet in a secluded area.
Don't let them try to get you in a hotel room. Now this sounds like common sense, but let me tell you something: they try. The guys are very cunning and crafty with their words. BE

CAREFUL and use discernment. Tell someone you love where you are going.

5. Beware of the married/separated man.
They will try you. Fact of the matter is they are still married, and that's tricky water you don't need to splash. Just say no. No man is *that* fine ladies. What is fine about someone who does not understand the word *commitment*?! I had a guy say he was married, not happy, and the wife was out of town. He wanted to meet at a hotel

blank stare

I hit the block button so quick. He didn't even deserve a response.

Love is a beautiful journey where wisdom should be taken along with you for the ride. You want to bring God into all relationships and let Him guide the way. It's been easier for me to stop and pray about someone versus going with the flow.

I wanted to share these tips with you because online dating has been a huge success. Even for those in my family. Yet I want you to be safe. We live in a world where the Internet is not always used for a pure purpose. Be prayerful and be aware mentally not just emotionally.

Conclusion

I had my wants. God had my needs. It's normal for women to desire the love, protection, and affection of a man. The first assignment a woman was given was to help a man. I desired what I had always lacked from my natural father. I looked for it in men. Through this journey not only did I find my way back to God, but my natural daddy as well. Father wounds have to be dealt with so you can heal and move forward. Today I understand. Heart break led me to forgive my natural father. I'll share more details in a later book.

God saw that man shouldn't be alone. Man, was not alone when Eve was created. God made the earth, planted the trees, formed animals, and let man name them. But there was still something missing. Man, needed someone to help him. So, God formed the women from his rib. God brought the woman out of the man so she can be the closest to him, to understand him, and to be him just as he is her.

What if your man has everything he needs? Career, home, savings, and all things that frame our world—except a woman? What if you are holding up his next level because you haven't decided to fully obey God? Your Adam could just be sleeping and God is just waiting to bring you too him. Did Mary wait for justification in order to act in strength and devotion? No. She had submitted far before the trial had begun.

Then the Lord God said, "It is not good for the man to be alone. I will make a helper who is just right for him." So the Lord God formed from the ground all the wild animals and all the birds of the sky. He brought them to the man to see what he would call them, and the man chose a name for each one. He gave names to all the livestock, all the birds of the sky, and all the wild animals. But still there was no helper just right for him. So the Lord God caused the man to fall into a deep sleep. While the man slept, the Lord God took out one of the man's ribs and closed up the opening. Then the Lord God made a woman from the rib, and he brought her to the man.

(Genesis 2:18-22)

The purist to finding acceptation after years of rejection isn't by putting yourself in more situations to be rejected. You cannot date yourself to a happy life. I was a helper to all my relationships—I found those men. I let myself serve them. But I was serving the wrong purpose, and from that I faced hardship. Striving to become pious woman does not mean servitude or that you are weaker or a maid—it means acting with God at the center of your decisions, relationships, and thoughts. If God is centered in your life, your man will have no reason to be upset with you or wander, unless he is weak of faith. By holding ourselves to a higher degree, we immediately hold men to an even higher standard. But if we do not value ourselves, men will not value us. And they will no longer value their purpose on this earth and begin to weight things through material and selfish considerations. And if he is weak of faith, you can help him build strength, but ultimately each soul has its own journey.

I hope this book opened your eyes to the idols you may have put in your life before God. I was trying to self-cure rejection; yours could be food, TV, social media, your family, or career. Whatever it is, take today to decide that you will no longer let that thing be more important than God. The only limits you have are the ones you've developed in your mind. Learn to affirm yourself daily with "I am" statements.

I am Amazing

I am Powerful

I am an achiever

I am an overcomer

I am a child of King Jesus

I can and will do all things God has called me to do!

Find your power and never let it go. I love you all thank you for being a part of my journey.

About the Author

Born and raised in Hillside, New Jersey Jennifer Mason left New Jersey to study business Marketing at North Carolina Central University. She also is a certified medical clinical assistant, entrepreneur, coach, mentor, sister, friend, and daughter. But of the title she holds is Woman of God.

Jennifer's mission is to inspire and build up women (young and old) to walk by faith, to always have confidence that their "right-now" doesn't have to be their forever. Doing this all with faith, class, experience and most importantly love.

Keep up with Jennifer Mason by visiting her website, www.jennifermichellem.com